HISTORY AND ORIGIN OF ALBERTA CONSTITUENCIES

Austin Mardon

Catherine Mardon

Edited by Aala Abdullahi

By Austin Mardon

International Law and Space Rescue Systems 1991;

Kensington Stone and Other Essays 1991;

A Transient in Whirl 1991;

Alone Against the Revolution 1996;

Political Networks in Alberta 1905-1992 2002;

7 days in Moscow 2005;

The Contribution of Geography to the Recovery of Antarctic Meteorites 2005;

History and Origin of Alberta Constituencies

Austin Mardon & Catherine Mardon

With Editing By

Aala Abdullahi

A Golden Meteorite Press Book.

© 2011 copyright by Austin Mardon, Edmonton, Canada.
All rights reserved. No part of this work may be reproduced in any form or by any means, electronic or mechanical, including photocopying, recording, taping, or any retrieval system, without the written permission of Golden Meteorite Press at aamardon@yahoo.ca.
No part of this publication may be reproduced, stored in a retrieval system or transmitted, in any form or by any means, without prior written consent of the publisher or a licence from The Canadian Copyright Licensing Agency (Access Copyright). For an Access Copyright licence, visit www.accesscopyright.ca or call toll free to 1-800-893-5777.

Cover design Pauline Balogun, 2011

Published by Golden Meteorite Press.
126 Kingsway Garden
Post Office Box 34181,
Edmonton, Alberta, CANADA.
T5G 3G4
Web site: www.austinmardon.org

ISBN 978-1-897472-29-3

Library and Archives Canada Cataloguing in Publication

Mardon, Austin A. (Austin Albert)
  History and origin of Alberta constituencies / Austin Mardon, Catherine Mardon ; edited by Aala Abdullahi.

ISBN 978-1-897472-29-3

  1. Election districts--Alberta--History. 2. Politicians--Alberta--Biography. 3. Alberta--Politics and government--20th century. I. Mardon, Catherine A., 1962- II. Abdullahi, Aala III. Title.

JL333.M29 2011   328.3'345097123   C2011-904740-3

Introduction

Statesmen, From and For Alberta

Before proceeding with the political history and development of each constituency and short biographical sketches of those who functioned for the state and ruled us, which is the burden of this study, it would seem proper and necessary to present a sketch of the apparatus of state in which they functioned. In that way, we may appreciate them and their contribution to our welfare all the more, through understanding the function they performed and the power they wielded for us on behalf of the state they served.

Canada, since the passage of the British North America Act (BNA) by the Parliament of the United Kingdom and the Proclamation by Queen Victoria of July 1st, 1867 as Confederation Day, is a federal state comprising two levels of constitutionally established government for the same Canadian citizen. On the one hand there is a national or federal representative Parliament in Ottawa, comprising the Crown personalized in the reigning monarch or the Governor General appointed by her on the advice of her Privy Council for Canada [effectively the federal Cabinet], the Senators and the Supreme Court Justices appointed by the Governor-General-in-Council, as well as the members of the House of Commons, elected by all Canadian citizens from specific geographically defined areas called federal ridings amongst whom is the Prime Minister and most of his Ministers, who constitute his Ministry or the federal Executive Council. On the other hand there is a provincial representative government in the capital of the now ten Canadian provinces, comprised of a Lieutenant-Governor who, with the justices of the superior courts of the province, is appointed by Ottawa, and the members elected periodically to the provincial Legislative Assembly by the residents of specific geographical constituencies into which the province has been divided and re-divided as population warranted. These are our M.L.A.s.

Because Canada is a constitutional monarchy, a democracy but not a republic, there is again a division of function and authority at both the federal and provincial levels consisting and authority at both the federal and provincial levels consisting of an amalgam of the Crown and the elected representatives. The Crown reigns and the elected members rule. Traditionally the Legislative and Executive branches of the State at both federal and provincial levels exist solely as advisors to the Crown in whom the ultimate authority of the State resides. Thus, at the federal level we have a Governor-General appointed by the reigning Monarch by Letters Patent, which since 1947 transmit to him as representative of practically all prerogatives of reign, viz: the right to act as Head of State for Canada in all foreign or domestic relations and to be commander-in-chief of the Canadian Armed Forces, receive ambassadors and proclaim war or peace; the right to grant Royal Pardon; the right to appoint Senators and Justices of the Supreme and Federal Courts as well as of superior courts in the provinces; but especially the right to call the leader of the majority political party returned at a general federal election to form a Cabinet, Executive Council, government or ministry of which he will be the Prime Minister and to swear in the Individual Ministers he has chosen to head the various ministries of Departments of his government, as well as remove them; the duty to accept the resignation of a Prime Minister, whose ministry has lost majority support for his policies, especially those concerning financial matters in the House of Commons or whose maximum five year term of office has expired and issue writs for a general election whenever the Prime Minister requests it; the right, between general elections to open and close Sessions of Parliament and be available to the Prime Minister for consultation concerning the policy his Ministry will adopt and the legislation and enactment they will introduce to realize it; to encourage and to warn him of foreseen difficulties in the name of the Crown on behalf of the citizenry, and finally to sanction all Acts or legislation passed by Parliament or Orders, Writs, Proclamations or Appointments, etc. prepared by the Executive for his signature in order that thereby they will acquire the "force of law", --- but never, never publicly propose any legislation or direction of policy himself or enter the political arena as the public protagonist of opinions or policies other than those espoused by Her Majesty's government and passed by Parliament.

At the provincial level we have a simplified version of a similar arrangement between the Crown and the elected members. We have a Lieutenant Governor appointed by the Governor-General in Council for each province, whose functions are similar to those of the Governor-General at the federal level except that he may withhold approval of doubtful provincial Legislation, Executive Orders, Proclamations, Writs or Warrants, etc. until the Federal Executive will have had an opportunity to study them and their implications for the Nation, then either disallow them, refer them to the Supreme Court of Canada for a ruling on their validity or allow them to become law. He can be removed from office by the Federal, but once he has been appointed derives his authority of office from the Constitution and Privy Council decisions thereon, whereby he becomes the manifestation of the Crown in his own province and official Head of State there. He is no longer a local superintendant of provincial affairs for the Federal Executive that appointed him.

He too calls upon the leader of the party which won the last provincial general election, the Premier, to form his governing Ministry or Cabinet; he swears them in as Ministers of the Executive Council, most of them heads of Departments of Government; he opens and closes Sessions of the Legislative Assembly, sanctions all legislation passed there, as well as all proclamations, writs, warrants, etc. prepared by the Executive Council for his signature including those calling for a general election or a by-election, but, even more so than his federal counterpart, must never state publicly or endorse any policy, legislation or enactment other than those of his government.

And so we see that at both the federal and provincial levels, the Crown reigns and the majority political party of elected members rules as Her Majesty's government and the minority party or parties as Her Majesty's equally loyal Opposition under a Prime Minister at the federal and a Premier at the Provincial level. The Crown, above politics, becomes the principle and force for unity in the State at both levels, since debates in the House or the Assembly on policy, legislation or direction, based as they are on the "adversary principle" can become quite vehement and create disunity even divisiveness amongst those who in their totality are the real rulers in the state; our elected representatives.

These members are generally elected on a political party basis by a majority vote of the residents of each particular geographical conscription riding for federal or constituency for provincial members on Election Day.

Thereby the residents of that area are deemed to have endorsed the election platform of their candidate, which he or his party hammered out and adopted and which he and other party spokesmen have presented to make supports of the residents and which he too is pledged to realize for them should he be elected.

These party platforms are intended to counteract flamboyant Public Relations and lower the amount of "impulse voting" which is based solely on a candidate's aura or charisma as manifested in personal or media appearances or is based exclusively on local issues or "gut" issues of race, religion or language or the like, which unfortunately in the present as in the past usually wins or loses the election, even in this enlightened ad electronic age. "Anything goes: to win a supporter on Election Day.

Political parties have an indispensable role to play at election time and during actual governing. Without them, it would be difficult to ensure any sort of continuous policy for development at either level of government, to know who in fact won a general election and by virtue of party-solidarity of members after caucus discussion, will ensure the government of majority support in the House or Assembly for its allotted five year span. Without political parties we would have a seriously reduced or indeed an entire "wipe-out" of supporters at the 'grass-roots' level,, who now nominate candidates and contribute ideas, public relations and financial support for the ensuing campaign. Third parties tend to rely more heavily upon the effective functioning of their local machinery, whereas the major parties generally dust them of only when a general election seems imminent, but they exist to ensure that a candidate will be chosen to sponsor an adaptation of the political party's known philosophy to the "here-and-now". They may not be constitutionally recognized, but are plain common and a necessary Convention of the life and stability of representative democracy.

Now because both levels of government, the federal and provincial, each one sovereign and independent of the other in their exclusive areas of competence, are both concerned with the common weal of the same citizen in the commonwealth, there can be conflict and there is certainly always tension in the pursuit of the objectives. In order that this tension might be minimized or at least remain controllable, the BNA Act has attempted to spill out the areas of competence or jurisdiction for each level. This it has done principally in Sections 91, 92 and 93 as originally drafted and since then as clarified by judicial decision or subsequent legislative addition or amendment. At the present point-in-time, discussion of areas of jurisdiction is a cave of winds.

As guidelines, it might nevertheless be conceded that the provincial governments have been charged with ensuring the <u>social</u> wellbeing of their immediate constituency through enactments dealing primarily with "property and Civil rights", and that the federal government is charged with the "Nation's business". By virtue of Section 91, the federal is empowered to "make laws for the Peace, Order and good Government in Canada" for the nation as a unified whole, and in specified categories named in this Section as well as all areas not assigned by Section 92 to the exclusive responsibility of their level, except for the right to denominational schools which is Magistrates or judges of their own provincial courts.

When Alberta became a province in 1905 the provincial government carried forward the court format which it had inherited form the Northwest Territories and the federal confirmed in office for the province those who had been judges in territorial courts there. Thus, we had a Chief Justice of the Supreme Court of Alberta which was divided into Trial and Appellate Divisions, and district courts for territorially determined areas as the same implies, whose presiding officers were known, not as justices, but as judges (even as were those of provincial courts), although they were appointed by the Federal government and with the justices, who were also so any kind even to the point of losing their voting franchise upon appointment to the Bench.

Above the provincial framework of courts was the Supreme Court of Canada constituted by statute and staffed by appointees of the federal government, who handled cases of both public and of private law, civil or criminal, either in the first instance or upon appeal from provincial or Court of Exchequer jurisdictions (public law are those concerned with the validity of statutes, existing or proposed by the federal). The final and last Court of Appeal for Canadians was the Judicial Committee of the Privy Council in London.

When appeals to the Privy Council were abolished in 1949, (Criminal cases 1933) the role of court of Last Resort was passed back to the Supreme Court of Canada. This added greatly to its scope and forced a restricting of criminal cases or civil cases in private law which it could hear. Ultimately, it would seem destined to become principally the final interpreter of statute law from either federal or provincial levels or arbiters in conflicts between the two levels and final Court of Appeal for legitimated and accepted cases from provincial Supreme Courts, but, hopefully not to the extent that the Supreme Court in the U.S. is active in protecting the Constitutional Bill of Rights from being infringed upon by National or State Legislatures to the point of even determining ways and means by which these entrenched Rights will be enhanced for the citizenry. Our Conventional Canadian view of Judges is that they must remain independent of politics in their decisions, must never enter into the political arena in any partisan way themselves in order to be better able to judge and interpret and apply laws or enactments made by the legislative or Executive branches at both the federal and provincial levels dispassionately and justly ascending to the "rule of law" for the benefit of all.

This Court framework was substantially altered for Alberta in 1971, when the formerly Appellate Division became the Supreme Court of Alberta, with more Justices named to that Bench. The former trial Division was merged with the district courts, to become a new Court of Queen's Bench, and the scope of provincial Courts was also widened. Still, because these provincial courts remain courts of the first instance and concerned with civil and criminal law cases there, we have in the study restricted our research to the federally appointed incumbents of the Bench in the higher courts if the province and the Supreme Court of Canada.

Such then is a bird's eye view of our apparatus of state as it appears to a layman who is not a constitutional lawyer. The question of power or authority, its origin and exercise has always fascinated and intrigued me; when this study of the proponents of power for the State in its three branches at its two levels. I have tried to write a short but pithy biography of each of these men in order that we might know more about them and their function. His study is of course only an initial first introduction of them to the reader and hopefully it will be followed by other researchers who will provide us with more detailed biographies of at least the more outstanding leaders among them. Nevertheless, it is hoped that the beginnings we have gathered here will provide the reader with a nearer look at the men and women who filled these roles of power for the state and for the common good of all of us: Canadians and Albertans.

The Constituency of Acadia

1913 – 1963

The Constituency of Acadia disappeared from the Alberta Electoral map in 1963 after existing fifty years. Nova Scotians who homesteaded in the Oyen district named their post office Acadia Valley in 1910. The name used in 1913 for the new constituency north of the South Saskatchewan River in the eastern part of the province. In 1924, the same name was used for the new federal riding north of Medicine Hat.

A total of six residents represented Acadia in the provincial house. The first was Liberal John McColl, who was a prosperous Colholme farmer that came west from Glengarry County, Ontario. He sat for eight years in the House as a private member. McColl retired from politics at the age of sixty-five.

In 1921, Lorne Proudfoot, the UFA candidate was elected, defeating the Liberal candidate by a majority of 2,200. He had contested unsuccessfully this constituency four years before. He was a prominent Chinook farmer who lived well up into his nineties. He sat in the Legislature for fourteen years as a private member.

In the 1935 general election, Social Creditor Norman B. James was elected. Born in England, he became a successful farmer in the Youngstown district. By 1940, James had bought himself a house in Edmonton and was returned as one of the five member "elected-at-large" in the Alberta Capital.

His successor of the member for Acadia was another Social Creditor, C.E. Gerhart, an Ontario-born accountant and chemist. He had served three terms as Mayor of Coronation. He sat in the Legislature for fifteen years. In 1943, Premier Manning appointed Gerhart to the Cabinet as the Minster of Municipal Affairs. He also was the Minister of Trade and Commerce and from 1948 to 1955 the Provincial Secretary for his last three years in the Legislature, he sat beside his son Edgar Gerhart, Social Credit member for Edmonton. This is the only occasion when a father and son sat together in the same Legislature in Alberta. Gerhart was forced to retire when defeated at the polls at the age of fifty-eight.

In the 1955 general election, Acadia went Liberal, electing James Sims, a Veteran farmer and garage operator. He sat only four years in the Legislature.

The last resident of this constituency to be sent to the Legislature was SoCred Marion Kelts. Born in 1980 at pelican Rapids, Minnesota, he was educated in North Dakota before homesteading near Consort. He served on the Consort school board as chairman for a number of years. He was sixty-eight years of age when he was first elected in the 1959 general election. Kelts retired from politics when the constituency of Acadia was joined to Hand Hills prior to the 1963 general lection.

These six pioneer farmers are remembered today as being public spirited, hard working men who served the citizens of Acadia well in the Legislature.

The Constituency of Alexandra
1909 – 1971

The former constituency of Alexandra first appeared on the Alberta Electoral Division Map in 1909. Sixty-nine years later it disappeared, being renamed Lloydminster. Why it was given the name of Alexandria is not known. The British Barr Colonist settled in this district.

A total of five men were elected for this constituency. The first was a wealthy young Englishman, A. Bramley-Moore, who was an outspoken critic of the federal government. He sat for four years in the House as a private Liberal Member. In 1911, he wrote: Canada and Her Colonies – home Blue for Alberta. He did not seek re-election in 1913. Bramley-Moore, was killed at Vimy Ridge while serving in the Canadian Army in 1917.

The second member for Acadia was Conservative James R. Lowery. He had run against Bramley-Moore in 1909 and after being defeated, had studied at Queen's University. He was a "student-at-law" when he entered the Legislature. He was the youngest member in the House and served as the Tory Junior Whip.

At the outbreak of World War I, Lowery joined the Canadian Army. In 1997, he was seriously wounded at Vimy Ridge while serving as a Major of the 151st Battalion. He sat for eight years in the Legislature before retiring from politics. Later, he became a Calgary lawyer and successful Calgary oil executive. He died of a heart attack while watching the Shriners football game in Vancouver in 1956.

In 1921, Peter Enzenauer, a Kitscoty rancher, was elected the UFA member. He had the largest majority of any member in the province. He had the largest majority of any member in the province. Born in the States, he homesteaded in the Vulcan district in 1904. He only had a grade four education, but this did not prevent him from inventing various farm machinery. He sat in the Legislature for fourteen years before being forced to retire from politics after being defeated at the polls.

The net member was Social Crediter Selmer Berg, an American-born Marwayne merchant. He was a member of the so-called "insurgents" who in 1937 attempted to topple the government of Premier Aberhart. Berg wanted Dr. Harvey Brown, the member for Lac Ste. Anne to become Premier. He sat for thirteen years as a private member before retiring from politics at the age of sixty-two.

The last member to represent Alexandra in the Legislature was Social Creditor Andrew Aalborg., who was born in 1914 at McLaughlin, Alberta of Norwegian parents.

The Constituency of Barrhead
1971 – Present

The Constituency of Barrhead was created from the old ridings of Lac Ste. Anne and Pembina prior to the 1971 general election. It reaches from Lac Ste. Anne, west of Edmonton to the 18th Base Line, a few miles south of Lesser Slave Lake. The main centre of population is the town of Barrhead with 3.332 residents, located on the Paddle River.

The first member of the Legislature was Dr. Hugh Horner, who had previously sat for Lac Ste, Anne. Born in 1925 at Blaine Lake, Saskatchewan, he is the second son of the late Senator Ralph Horner. He was educated at the University of Saskatchewan and obtained a Medical degree from the University of Western Ontario. He then established himself as a physician at Barrhead. Horner sat for nine years as the Member of Parliament for Jasper Edson, before entering provincial politics. He contested successfully Lac Ste. Anne in 1967 by defeating incumbent SoCred William Patterson.

In 1971, when Premier Lougheed formed his first Cabinet, he named Horner the Deputy Premier and the Minister of Agriculture. Four years later, he was transferred from Agriculture to Transportation. Following the 1979 general election, he was appointed to the economic development portfolio. However, in November of the same year, he resigned his seat in order to take a senior position in the federal civil service.

The resulting November 21, 1979 by-election, was the only one besides Olds/Didsbury, held during the life of the 19th Alberta Legislature.

Ken Kowalski, held the seat for the Conservative but only by a narrow 355 margin in a four way contest. The runner-up was Liberal Alberta leader, Nick Taylor. Born in 1945 at Bonnyville, Kowalski was educated at the University of Alberta before becoming a school teacher. In 1975, he became Dr. Horner's executive assistant, and held this position until he entered provincial politics.

The November 2nd general election will be a replay of the 1979 by-election with Kowalski being again opposed by Nick Taylor. Born in 1927 at Bow Island, Taylor is the son of Frederick Taylor, a native of Newcastle, New Brunswick, and Marie Ancion of Liege, Belgium. Educated at St. Theresa's College, Medicine Hat, he obtained a degree in Science from the University of Alberta. He became a successful geologist and millionaire Calgary oil man with petroleum interests in the North Sea oil field and the Middle East.

In 1974, he was chosen the Alberta leader of the Liberal party. Since then, he has attempted unsuccessfully to enter the Legislature on four occasions. Kowalski was re-elected in the November 1982 general election.

The Constituency of Bonnyville
1952 – 1982

The constituency of Bonnyville was created prior to the 1952 general election. This North east region of the province was opened up to French settlement in 1907. The promoter was Rev. Bonny, O.M.I., after whom the town of Bonnyville, with a population of 3,100, is named.

The first member was Laudas Jolly, the former member for St. Paul. He was returned as a UFA member in the 1920's and as "Social Crediter in the 1950's." He retired from politics in 1955 at the age of sixty-seven.

In 1955, Bonnyville elected Liberal Jake Josvanger, a Beaver Crossing merchant and farmer. He was a member of the largest opposition that Premier Manning was ever faced: There were thirty-seven government members versus twenty-four on the opposition benches. Josvanger was defeated in his re-election bid after sitting in the Legislature for four years.

In 1959, the Social Credit recaptured the constituency when Karl Nordstrom was elected. Two years later, the forty-one year old St. Paul farmer died unexpectedly.

In the resulting November 1961 by-election, Social Crediter Romeo Lamothe was elected. He sat for ten years in the Legislature as a private member. Born in 1914 at St. Paul, he was educated at Edmonton's St. John College before attending Camrose Normal School.

After teaching for five years, he briefly operated the St. Paul Co-op before joining the Canadian Air Force at the outbreak of World War II. He saw active duty as a flight lieutenant in Northwest Europe. On his return to Canada, Lamothe purchased the Bonnyville general store. He served as a school trustee and a town councillor before entering provincial politics.

In the 1971 general election, Tory Donald Hansen was elected by defeating SoCred Lorne Mowers. He represented the constituency or eight years as a private member.

The present member for Bonnyville in the Legislature is Ernest Isley, a forty-six year old insurance agent and farmer. Educated at Kitscoty, he attended the University of Alberta before teaching in Vermillion. He was the principal of the Bonnyville Regional High School when elected to the Legislature three years ago.

The Constituency of Bow Valley
1913 – 1982

The large Southern Alberta constituency of Bow Valley is located between the Red Deer River to the north and the Bow/South Saskatchewan River to the south. It was established in 1913 by cutting off the eastern half of the constituency of Gleichen. The largest centre of population is Brooks with 8,000 residents. The first member elected in Bow Valley was Liberal George Lane who, with A.J. McLean and Pat Burns, organized the first Calgary Stampede in 1912. However, Lane resigned before taking his seat in the Legislature to permit Attorney General C.R. Mitchell to re-enter the House. In the general election, Mitchell had been defeated in neighboring Medicine Hat by Tory, Nelson Spencer by 15 votes. Mitchell was returned by acclamation and represented this constituency for the next thirteen years until he was re-appointed a judge.

In the 1926 general election, candidates were Captain Joseph T. Shaw, the Liberal Alberta leader, Ben Plumer, a director of the UFA and Tory, Edmund Purcell. Captain Shaw (1883 – 1944), who was a former Calgary Member of parliament, was finally declared elected by the courts with a majority of one. Shaw retired from politics to practice law in Calgary in 1930.

The next member was Independent John MacKintosh. He did not seek re-election in 1935. Bow Valley elected SoCred W.E. Cain in 1935 and he represented the constituency as a private member for the next twenty years. He was forced to retire from politics in 1955 when defeated at the polls. He was sixty-eight years of age.

His successor was SoCred William Deday. Social Creditor Fred Manderville, who sat in the House for eighteen years, did not seek re-election in the November 1982 general election.

The Constituency of Cardston

The Constituency of Cardston is situated in the southwest corner of Alberta. In the late 1980's a large group of members of the Church of Jesus Christ of Latter Day Saints (Mormons), moved north from their homes in Utah to establish a colony in the Canadian Northwest Territories.

They were led by the pioneer Mormon leader Charles Ora Carol, son-in-law of Brigham Young.

In 1905, Cardston elected Liberal John Woolf, who had represented the district in the NWT Assembly at Regina. Woolf (1868 – 1950) was a prominent pioneer Mormon rancher. In 1910, he returned to the States in order to work full-time for his Church. The Legislature declared seat vacant and a by-election was called for May 1912. John's elder brother, Martin Woolf, was returned and sat in the Legislature for nine years. Martin Woolf (1858 – 1928) was named the Deputy Speaker of the Legislature. He was also a successful pioneer farmer and rancher. He was forced to retire from politics after being defeated at the polls in 1921 at the age of sixty-two.

George L. Stringham held the seat for fourteen years for the UFA. Born in 1876 in Utah, he came north as a young man to Alberta and became a successful farmer of the Glenwoodville district. His son, Bryce Stringham, was the Independent member for Bow Valley in the 1950's.

The fourth member to represent Cardston in the Legislature was Nathan Eldon Tanner, one of the prominent Albertans alive today. Born in 1900 in Utah, he came to Alberta with his parents as a child. He was educated at the Calgary Normal School before becoming a teacher at Spring

Hill in 1917. He remained there for ten years before becoming the principal of the Cardston High School. He held this position for eight years. He also served on the Cardston town council. Tanner was appointed the Mormon bishop of the Cardston ward and was active in the church.

In 1935, he was elected the Social Credit member for Cardston and sat in the Legislature for the next seventeen years. He was named the Speaker in 1936 and the next year joined Premier Aberhart's cabinet as the Minister of Lands and Mines. Today, Tanner is given credit for encouraging American petroleum companies to explore for oil and natural gas in Alberta. The result of this exploration was the discovery of the Leduc oil field in 1947. The oil revenues changed Alberta from a "have not" province.

In 1952, Tanner retired from politics to become a successful businessman. He was, for several years, the president of Trans Canada Pipe Lines. For the past twenty years, he has devoted his life to church work and is now one of the leaders of the Mormon Church. He lives in Salt Lake City, Utah.

The next member was Edgar Hinman, who has sat for Cardston from 1952 to 1967 and again from 1971 to 1975. Born in 1906 in Cardston, he was educated as a teacher. He holds a Masters degree from Brigham Young University. In the 1920's and 1930's, Hinman was associated with three other teachers, Nathan Tanner, Solon Low – National leader of the Social Credit and John Blackmore – long-time MP for Lethbridge. He later served as a superintendent of schools for the Department of Education. In 1955, Premier Manning took him into the cabinet as the Provincial Treasurer. He held the position for nine years. Hinman finally retired from politics in 1975 at the age of sixty-nine.

Prior to the 1967 general election, Hinman lost the Social Credit nomination to Alvin Bullock. At the time, the Kirby Inquiry was examining the alleged misconduct of Hinman while he was in the cabinet. Born at Welling, Bullock was educated at Raymond. He has spent two and one half years in the Mormon missions. He also spent twenty years as a Mormon bishop. He operated the large family farm near Welling. He did not seek re-election in 1971, but let Hinman be returned.

The Incumbent member for Cardston is Tory John Thompson, a Spring Coulee farmer. Born in 1924 at Pasadena, California, he was educated at Magrath before attending the University of Alberta and the East Texas State Teachers College. In 1949, he married Le Vaun Matkin of Magrath. In the November 2nd general election, Thompson was re-elected, defeating the efforts of the Western Canada Concept candidate to capture the seat.

The Constituency of Chinook
1979 – 1982

The largest Central Alberta Constituency of Chinook lies north of the Red Deer River near the Saskatchewan border. The main centre populations are Hanna – 2,600; Coronation – 1,300; and Oyen – 1,000. It was created prior to the 1979 general election by merging Hanna/Oyen with Sedgewick/Coronation. This constituency is in the Alberta portion of the dry-lands of the Palliser Triangle.

The member for Chinook is Henry Kroeger, a Russian0born sixty-five year old Consort farmer and businessman. He came to Alberta with his parents in 1926 and completed his education at Consort. Kroeger farmed in the 1930's and 1940's before establishing a farm equipment firm in Consort. He opened a branch at Stettler in 1952.

Always interested in politics, he was the unsuccessful Liberal candidate for Stettler in 1959. After being active in the Liberal party for twenty years, he joined the Conservatives. He was first elected to the Legislature as the Conservative member for Sedgewick/Coronation in 1975, by defeating the incumbent SoCred Ralph Sorenson. Four years later, he won the nomination for Chinook by edging out Jack Butler, the incumbent PC member for Hanna/Oyen.

In the 1979 general election Kroeger had a 2,700 vote majority over his nearest opponent, SoCred Arlie Reil. After this election, Premier Lougheed named him to the Cabinet as the Minister of Transportation.

Kroeger was re-elected in the November 2nd general election. He is one of the most outspoken and colorful members of the Legislature.

The Former Constituency of Clearwater
1913 – 1925

The large constituency of Clearwater first appeared on the Alberta Electoral Division Map in 1913 and disappeared in 1925 when a special Act of the Legislature abolished it. The descriptive name comes from a tributary of the North Saskatchewan River. It first appeared on Thompson's Map of Western Canad, published in 1814.

The well known pioneer Albertans represented this constituency in the Legislature; Henry W. McKenney and Dr. J.E. State.

In the April 17, 1913 general election, McKenney, who had sat as the Liberal member for both St. Albert and Pembina was elected by one vote! He had forty votes to Conservative A. Williamson Taylor's 39 an Socialist Joseph A. Clarke's 24. However, there were only 80 voters on the Voter's List.

Both Williamson Taylor and Clarke appealed the decision in the courts. Judge Noel ordered an official recount to be held before him on May 23. But McKenney went himself to court and persuaded Mr. Justice N.D. Beck of the Supreme Court to issue a writ Mandamur, cancelling the recount. Next, Williamson Taylor's lawyers were successful in getting Mr. Justice Beck's decision reversed by the Supreme Court's Appeal division. The date for the recount was reset for August 23, and then moved to August 30. The sheriff requested John McKerracher, the Clearwater Returning Officer, to produce the ballot boxes that had been sealed after being counted on the night of the election back in April.

But by this time, McKerracher had given the ballot boxes to Donald Baker, clerk of the Executive Council, and departed for a holiday in Ontario. Baker appeared in court after being subpoenaed, but refused to hand over the ballots to the judge, stating that as clerk of the Executive Council, he was responsible to the Legislature, not the courts. Judge Noel declared to find Baker in contempt of Court. Williamson Taylor appealed to the Supreme Court, which ruled in October that Baker was perhaps guilty of poor judgment but not of contempt; then, the two defeated candidates dropped the case. It was discovered that members of a surveying crew had voted which was legal. Taylor's lawyers appealed and by the end of the summer, the recount was scheduled to be held before Judge Beck.

However, by that time, the Clearwater Returning Officer ad handed over the ballot boxes to the clerk of the Executive Council. He refused to hand over the ballot boxes, maintaining that a District Court Judge had no power over a Superior Court, the Legislative Assembly in this case. The result was that there was never an official recount. McKenney sat in the House for a total of twelve years for three different constituencies before retiring in 1917 at the age of seventy.

Liberal Joseph Ephraim State was born in Ontario, and educated at the Detroit Medical College before coming to Alberta. He homesteaded in the Fort Assiniboine district while remaining an "on call" doctor. Later, he became an Edmonton physician. It was said that Dr. State's practice consisted primarily of writing out prescriptions for liquor after prohibition was introduced. E was one of the most popular and most eccentric members. He sat for seven years in the house and died August 9, 1924 at the age of fifty-seven, while still a sitting member.

Rather than call a by-election, Premier Greenfield's government passed a special Act abolishing the constituency of Clearwater. This is the only time this happened in Alberta.

The Constituency of Clover Bar
1930 – 1982

The Constituency of Clover Bar was created prior to the 1930 general election. It is the area east of Edmonton. The largest community is Fort Saskatchewan with a population of more than 10,000. This constituency obtains its name from Thomas H. Clover (1809 – 1897), an American gold prospector, who panned for the precious metal in the North Saskatchewan in the 1860s.

A total of three residents have been elected to the provincial house in the past fifty-two years. The first was Rudolph Hennig, who had been the former UFA member for Victoria. Born in 1886 at Kischeneff, Russia, he came to Canada as a child with his parents. He was educated at Josephburg, near Edmonton, before becoming a successful farmer. He served for sixteen years as a school trustee before entering politics in 1926. He did not seek re-election in 1935 and died in 1969.

The second member for Clover Bar was Social Crediter Rev. Floyd Baker, a United Church minister, who sat in the Legislature for a total of twenty-eight years as a private member. In 1940, he was opposed by A.H. Gibson, who ran as an Independent. Three years before, while serving as an Edmonton police magistrate, Gibson sentenced Joseph Unwin, the Social credit member for Edson, to six months in prison as a result of authoring a pamphlet containing defamatory libel. The Aberhart government dismissed Gibson a few months later. Baker retired from politics in 1963 at the age of seventy-two.

The incumbent member for Clover Bar is SoCred Dr. Walter Buck, who has sat in the Legislature for eighteen years. Even though he had never served in the Cabinet, he contested unsuccessfully the Social Credit leadership when manning retired in 1968. Born in 1930 at Heinburg, Alberta, he attended the Camrose Lutheran College before obtaining a degree in dentistry from the University of Alberta. He had practiced as a dental surgeon at Fort Saskatchewan since 1955.

In the November 1982 general election, he was re-elected as an Independent. Currently, Dr. Buck is one of the four Opposition members of the 79 seat Legislature.

The Constituency of Cypress
1926 – 1982

The Constituency of Cypress first appeared on the Alberta Electoral Division Map when it was carved out of the two member Medicine hat riding prior to the 1926 general election. It is in the southeastern corner of the province with the South Saskatchewan River as its northern boundary. This constituency got its name from the Cypress Hills, which is the highest range of hills between the Labrador Highlands and the Rocky Mountains.

A total of five men and one woman have represented this constituency in the Legislature. The first member elected for Cypress was the UFA Minister of Education, Perrin Baker. He was a University educated Nemiskau farmer who had previously sat for Medicine Hat. He was defeated at the polls after sitting in the House for fourteen years.

The next member was Social Crediter August Flamme, an American-born Bow Island farmer. He served as a Forty Mile district councilor prior to entering provincial politics. He was defeated at the polls in 1940.

The next member was Independent Fay Jackson. In 1940, Fay Jackson was elected as an Independent. He was an American-born Etzikom merchant and implement dealer, who served as secretary/treasurer of the local school district for fifteen years. He retired from politics in 1944 at the age of fifty-six.

The fourth member was English-born Mrs. Edith Thurston, a Bow Island farmer's wife. She was the Social Credit member for one term. In 1948, she was unsuccessful in obtaining her party's nomination, being defeated by J.W.

Underdahl. Underdahl held the seat for Social Credit in the 1948 election. Underdahl had come to Alberta in 1910 from North Dakota. After two years in the RCMP, he was a police magistrate for twenty-two years before entering politics. He retired in 1955.

The sixth member was Harry Strom, a Burdett farmer, who represented Cypress from 1955 to 1975. Prior to entering the Legislature, he had served twenty-six years as a municipal councilor. In 1962, Premier Manning took Strom into his cabinet as Minister of Agriculture. When manning retired six years later, Strom became the Province's ninth Premier. He was the premier for three years. His administration was defeated in 1971, even though he personally was re-elected. He retired from politics in 1975 at the age of sixty-one.

This incumbent member for Cypress was Conservative Allan Hyland, a thirty-seven year old Bow Island farmer. He has sat in the House for eight years. Hyland was re-elected in the November 2nd general election.

The constituency of Cypress is the smallest in population of the largest area in Southern Alberta. It is likely that it will disappear as a result of redistribution prior to the next general election.

The Constituency of Drayton Valley

The Constituency of Drayton Valley was established prior to the 1971 general election from part of Stony Plain and Edson. The town of Drayton Valley, which has a population of 4,400, was first settled when there was a proposal to dam the North Saskatchewan River. The project was later abandoned. Rapid growth took place in the 1950s after discovery of the Pembina oil field. The main industry in this constituency is oil production and farming.

The first member for Drayton Valley was Tory Rudolph Zander, a Tomahawk farmer, who sat in the Legislature for eight years as a private member. Born in 1916 at Tomahawk, he was educated at Edmonton's Concordia Lutheran College. He served nineteen years as a Stony plain councilor before entering provincial politics. Zander retired in 1979 at the age of sixty-three.

The present member of the Legislature is Mrs. Shirley Cripps, a Westrose school teacher.

The Constituency of Drumheller
1930 – 1982

The Constituency of Drumheller is located in the "badlands" northeast of Calgary. It was originally established in 1930 because of the increase in population connected with the coal mining industry. Samuel Drumheller, an American businessman, purchased the townsite in 1912 and developed the coal field. Drumheller was incorporated as a city in 1930.

The first of the four members who have been elected to represent this constituency in the Legislature was lawyer Fred Moyer, who sat for five years as an Independent. He only defeated the Labor candidate newspaper editor A.F. Key, by 56 votes.

The second member was SoCred Herbert Ingrey, an English-born service station operator and cartage contractor, who was elected in the 1935 Social Credit landslide. In 1940, the Social Credit board and Premier Aberhart named Ingrey the party's candidate again because he was popular with the miners. However, the farmers selected a young school teacher, Gordon Taylor, to run as an Independent Social Crediter. "For the good of the party" Ingrey retired from politics.

Taylor was elected eleven times and sat as the member for Drumheller for a total of thirty-nine years. This is a record. Born in Calgary in 1910, he attended Calgary Normal School before becoming a teacher. During the Second World War, he served in the Air Force as a pilot officer.

He had a distinguished career in the Legislature. First, he was the Social Credit Party Whip from 1943 to 1950. Then, Premier Manning named him to the cabinet as the

Minister of Highways and Telephones. He held this portfolio for the next twenty years. He was the runner up to Harry Strom in the Social Credit leadership convention when Manning retired in 1968. Premier Strom re-appointed him to the cabinet.

In 1979, Taylor did not seek re-election to the Legislature, but moved into federal politics as the Conservative candidate for Bow River. He had a 17,000 majority in the 1979 federal election and increased it to 24,000 majority in 1980. In 1931, Taylor organized and still runs Camp Gordon, a camp for boys and girls not otherwise getting a holiday.

The present member for Drumheller is L.M. "Mickey" Clerk, an East Coulee farmer, who had a 3,600 vote majority over Independent Vern Hoff in the 1979 general election. Born in 1923 at Bassano, Clerk, son of an American pioneer rancher, was educated at Bassano High School before joining the Canadian Air Force during the Second World War. After leaving the service, he farmed in the Hussar district. Always interested in politics, he was elected to the Wheatland county council in 1972. He has served as the chairman of the Wheatland Board of Education and also chairman of the Drumheller General Hospital Board. Clerk was re-elected in the 1982 general election.

The Constituency of Edson

The Constituency of Edson was created from the western portion of St. Albert prior to the 1913 general election. It was named after the town of Edson, which has a population of 5,000 today. "Edson" Chamberlain, general manager of the Grand Trunk Pacific Railway, was the business responsible for the development of the coal mines in the Coal Branch field high in the Rockies south of the main east-west railway line. For many years, the majority of voters in this constituency were miners.

A total of eight residents have been elected to the Legislature in the past sixty-nine years. C.W. Cross, the Attorney General, was the first member. He had been in the provincial house since 1905 and has been the only person to sit for two constituencies – Edson and Edmonton – at the same time. Born in 1972 in Ontario, Cross educated at Toronto University and Osgoode Hall. He sat for twenty years in the Legislature until he resigned his seat in order to contest successfully the federal riding of Athabasca. In the 1926 federal election he was defeated by the UFA candidate, D.F. Kellner. He died in 1928.

In the Alberta general election of 1926, Christopher Pattinson, the Labor Candidate, was elected and held the Edson seat for nine years. Active in the Trade Union movement, he was an Englishman by birth and was educated at the Labor College, Oxford. Pattinson came to Alberta in 1911 to work in the Coal Branch mines.

In 1935, Social Crediter Joseph Unwin was elected. English born Edson salesman, he was immediately named his Party Whip in the Legislature. In 1937, Unwin with George Powell was arrested for writing and publishing the "Bankers

Toadies" pamphlet. He was convicted of defamatory libel and received a six month prison sentence, which he spent in the Fort Saskatchewan prison. Unwin has been the only member of the Legislature to be sent to prison while being a sitting member. He was defeated at the polls when he sought re-election.

In 1940, Edson elected Angus Morrison, the Labor candidate, who retired four years later. In the 1944 general election, SoCred Norman Willmore, an American-born Edson shoe merchant, was returned and held the seat in the Legislature until his death in an automobile accident in February 1965. He held two cabinet posts: Minister of Industries and Labour from 1953 to 1955 and then Minister of Lands and Forests.

In the resulting by-election, Liberal William Switzer was elected by a narrow 90 vote margin over the NDP leader Neil Reimer. Born in Edson, he joined the Air Force after leaving high school and saw active service as a fighter pilot in Western Europe. He is credited with the destruction of the car that Field Marshall Rommel was riding in and the serious wounding of the former Africa Corps General in July 1944. After the war, he qualified as a pharmacist. He was the Mayor of Hinton when he entered the Legislature. Like Willmore, Switzer was killed in an automobile accident in 1969 while still a sitting member.

In the second by-election of the decade, Tory Robert Dowling was elected and sat in the Legislature for the next ten years. In 1971, he entered Lougheed's first cabinet as the Minister without Portfolio responsible for Tourism, and later as the Minister of Consumer Affairs. After 1975, Dowling was appointed Minister of Development and Tourism. Born in 1924 at Camrose, he was a Canadian Air Force pilot during the war. He then attended the University of Alberta before becoming a pharmacist in Jasper. He retired from politics in 1979 at the age of fifty-five. Later, he was in charge of the province's 75th celebrations.

The incumbent member for Edson is Dr. Ian Reid, and English-born Hinton physician.

The nine men who have served the residents of Edson in the Alberta Legislature should be remembered as politically spirited men of ability.

The Constituency of Hand Hills

The Constituency of Hand Hills first appeared on the Alberta Electoral Division Map in 1913 and disappeared in 1971. The name is derived from the Hand Hills, north east of Calgary. According to legend, a Blackfoot chief was killed by the Cree in the early days in this locality. The chief had one small hand which by circumstance the name was given.

A total of four men represented this constituency in the Legislature during the fifty-eight years of its existence. The first was Robert B. Eaton, a Craigmyle farmer, who had served with the Canadian Mounted Rifles in the Boer War. He rejoined the army at the outbreak of World War I and saw active service on the Western Front. He sat in the House for eight years.

In the 1921 general election, G.A. Foster, the UFA candidate, was elected and sat in the House for fourteen years.

In the Social Credit sweep of 1935, Hand Hills returned Dr. W.W. Cross, a close personal friend of William Aberhart. He was immediately taken into the cabinet of premier Aberhart as the Minister of Health. He held his portfolio for the next twenty-four years. Dr. Cross retired in 1959 at the age of sixty-six.

The last person to hold this seat was Social Crediter, C. Keith French. He was a Hanna pharmacist who was Mayor of the Central Alberta town elected to the Legislature. He represented Hand Hills from 1959 to 1971 and then was returned as the member for Hanna/Oyen. He retired in 1975 at the age of sixty-eight. French was recognized as one of the ablest back benchers in the House. Many thought he should have been taken into the cabinet.

Hand Hills was well served by its members who were public spirited men over the years.

The Constituency of Innisfail
1905 – 1940
and
1971 – 1982

The Constituency of Innisfail was established prior to the first Alberta general election in November 1905, but it disappeared in the 1940 redistribution. It reappeared in 1971 when the city of Red Deer to the North started to grow in population. The town of Innisfail, which now has a population close to 6,000, was named after a town in Scotland in 1893.

The first member for Innisfail was John A. Simpson, a wealthy pioneer merchant and rancher, who had represented the district in the NWT Legislature at Regina. He won the election after the returning officer used his franchise to break a tie vote. Simpson sat in the Legislature for eight years until he was forced to retire after being defeated at the polls.

In the 1913 general election, Tory Fred Archer was elected by a narrow margin of nine votes. Born in 1859 in Ireland, he was educated in Dublin before coming to Canada as a young man. He served under Co. Bolton in a militia unit during the Riel Rebellion of 1885. Later, he became homesteaded near Innisfail and became a prosperous farmer.

In 1917, Liberal Daniel Morkeberg was elected, defeating Archer by 199 votes. Born in Denmark, he served in the Danish Royal Guards as a young man. In 1898, Morkeberg was on his way to the Klondike gold fields but did not get beyond Alberta. He homesteaded in the Markeville district. He was knighted by the King of Denmark in 1924 for his contribution to the dairy industry. He only sat in the Legislature for four years.

Donald Cameron was the UFA member for Innisfail for fourteen years. Born in Scotland, he worked as a shipwright with the British Admiralty in Hong Kong before becoming a pioneer homesteader near Elnora. (His son is Senator Donald Cameron of Banff).

Social Crediter A.E. McLellan represented this constituency from 1935 to 1940, when Innisfail disappeared from the Electoral Map. McLellan quit the Social Credit party to sit as an Independent in 1940. Redistribution resulted in the disappearance of Innisfail from 1940 to 1971 from the Electoral Map of Alberta.

In the 1971 general election, Tory Cliff Doan was elected in the resurrected constituency, defeating William Ure, the former Social Credit member for Red Deer by 320 votes. Doan sat for eight years in the Legislature as a private member. Born in 1905 at Halkirk, Alberta, he was a prominent Innisfail farmer for many years. He served as a Red Deer county councilor for twenty-six years. He retired from politics in 1979 at the age of seventy-four.

The member for Innisfail in the Legislature is Tony Nigel Pengally, a Delburne school principal and farmer.

The Constituency of Little Bow
1913 – 1982

The Constituency of Little Bow lies between the Bow River to the North and the Oldman River to the south. It is the heartland of the rich Wheatland of southern Alberta. The centre of population is Vulcan, with its long line of grain elevators. This region was settled by American homesteaders early in this century.

In the past seventy years, four individuals have represented Little Bow in the Legislature. First was James McNaughton (1864-1959), a wealthy, retired merchant who took up farming in the Carmangay district late in life. He sat as a private Liberal member for eight years.

The second member was O.L. "Tony" McPherson, an American-born Vulcan farmer. He sat in the Legislature for fourteen years- first as the Speaker, and then as Premier Brownlee's Minister of Public Works, McPherson was a colorful and controversial public figure. In the early 1930s, he was involved in a divorce scandal. Premier Reid did not include him in his short-lived administration. After being elected by acclamation in 1930, McPherson only obtained twenty percent of the vote five years later.

The third member to be sent to Edmonton was Rev. Peter Dawson (1892 – 1963), a Social Crediter who sat in the Legislature for twenty-eight years. He too was named the Speaker and served in this position for twenty-six years, a British Commonwealth record. Born in Ayrshire, Scotland, Dawson came to Alberta as a young man to train for the Ministry in Edmonton's St. Stephen's Theological College. He was the United Church minister at Carmangay for most of his life. He died in March 1963 while still a sitting member.

Little Bow's present member is SoCred Ray Speaker, the leader of the official Opposition. He is the dean of the House, having first been elected in 1963 at the age of twenty-eight. Born at Enchant within the constituency, he is the son of Michael Speaker, who came to Canada from Austria and Olga Christiansen of Norwegian-Danish descent. After obtaining an Education degree, he worked as a school teacher. He was taken into Premier Manning's Cabinet in 1967 as a Minister without Portfolio. He served as Premier Strom's Minister of Social Development.

Ray Speaker was re-elected as an Independent in 1982.

The Constituency of MacLeod
1884 – 1982

The first individual to be elected to NWT Legislative Assembly at Regina a hundred years ago from what was to become southern Alberta, was Viscount Bogle, the son of the Earl of Shannon. Bogle had served in the famous British regiment, the KRRC as an Officer prior to enlisting in the North West Mounted Police. After spending several years with the force, he became a prominent Macleod rancher, he was elected by acclamation to the Assembly. Viscount Bogle recruited a unit of Mounted Militia at the outbreak o the North West Revolt of 1885 and saw active service during the campaign. He was one of the few persons present at the hanging of Louis Riel in Regina in November 1885.

The next member for Macleod to sit in the NWT Legislature was Sir Frederick W. Haultain (1857 – 1942), who represented the constituency from 1888 to 1905. He was the premier for the last eight years of the Regina parliament. Haultain is recognized today as the individual who did most to persuade the federal government to create the provinces of Alberta and Saskatchewan in 1905.

The first member for Macleod in the Alberta Legislature was Malcolm McKenzie (1863 – 1913).

In 1909, MacKenzie decided to run in the new neighboring constituency of Claresholm. In Macleod, Liberal Colin Genge, a hotel proprietor, defeated Tory E.P. McNeil by 15 votes. (Four years later. McNeil was appointed a judge and served for twenty-seven years on the Alberta Bench). Genge never took his seat in the Legislature but died after a lengthy illness in March 1910.

In the resulting by-election, pioneer rancher Robert Patterson was elected. He sat as a Conservative for seven years.

In 1917, Liberal George Skedding contested successfully Macleod defeating Patterson by 50 votes.

In the 1921 general election, the UFA swept the Liberals out of office. Macleod returned William H. Shield, an English-born farmer, who held the seat for the next fourteen years.

In 1935, Social Crediter James Hartley defeated Shields in an upset victory. Born in 1888 in Yorkshire, England, he came to Canada as a young man and became a prominent Macleod rancher. He served a term on the Macleod town council.

Hartley sat for a total of thirty-two years in the Legislature. The first twenty as a private member before being appointed by Premier Manning to the Cabinet as the Minister of Public Works in 1955. He retired from politics in 1967 at the age of seventy-nine.

In 1967, SoCred Leighton Buckwell was elected and sat in the Legislature for eight years. He was a Raymond-born Macleod district rancher, who was a director of the Lethbridge Northern Irrigation district.

In 1975, Tory Dr. John Walker, contested the seat successfully defeating Buckwell by a 1.300 margin. Born in 1927 at Armagh, North Ireland, he graduated in Medicine from Trinity College, Dublin University before coming to Macleod in 1958. He was nicknamed "that Dam Doctor" for his stand on the construction of a large dam on the Oldman

River. In 1978, he failed to win his party's nomination and retired from politics.

The present member for Macleod is Tory Leroy Fjordbottem. Born in 1938 at Claresholm, he was educated at the Camrose Lutheran College before becoming a successful Granum farmer and rancher. In 1982, he was appointed to the Cabinet as Minister of Agriculture.

The Constituency of Medicine Hat
1905 – 1982

Prior to the creation of the province, Medicine Hat was in the district of Assiniboia.

In 1905, it returned Liberal W.T. Finlay, a British-born wealthy lumber merchant, who had represented the area in the NWT Assembly. Finlay was Alberta's first Provincial Secretary and Minister of Agriculture. In 1910, he resigned his seat due to failing health, and died two years later at the Coast.

In the resulting by-election, Liberal C.R. Mitchell, a former district judge, was elected. He went straight into Premier Sifton's Cabinet as the Attorney General. Mitchell failed in his bid for re-election in 1913.

Medicine Hat's third member of the Legislature was Conservative Nelson Spencer (1876 – 1943), a prominent city merchant and former Mayor. He held the seat for eight years, Col. Spencer commanded the 175th Battalion in France during World War I. He resigned to contest unsuccessfully the federal riding of Medicine hat in the 1921 by-election caused by the death of Secretary of State, Arthur Sifton.

In the January 19, 1961 election, SoCred Harvey Leinweber, a Russian-born life underwriter and former alderman, was elected and held the seat until he retired from politics in 1971.

The Former Constituency of Redcliff
1913 – 1921

The Constituency of Redcliff, which first appeared in the Alberta Electoral Map in 1913, was expected to grow in population. It was named after the town of Redcliff, which was referred to as the future "Pittsburgh of Alberta". The prophecy did not materialize and the constituency was abolished prior to the1921 general election.

The only member of the Legislature for the ill-fated Redcliff was Charles S. Pingle. Born in 1880 at Morris, Manitoba, he was educated in Winnipeg and then went to Regina where he was apprenticed as a druggist. He became a prominent Medicine Hat businessman.

Active in the Liberal party, he served a term as the Provincial President before contesting successfully in Redcliff in 1913.

At the outbreak of World War I, he joined the Canadian Army and served as an officer with the 3rd C.M.R. in France.

When the Speaker of the Legislature died in 1920, Captain Pingle was named to succeed him. He was defeated in the UFA sweep of 1921, but re-entered the House in the 1925 Medicine Hat by-election. He was pressured ot become the Alberta Liberal leader in 1926 when C.R. Mitchell was appointed a judge.

Captain Pingle died January 10, 1928 while still a sitting member at the age of fifty-eight.

He is remembered as one of the pioneer political leaders of Alberta.

The Constituency of Red Deer

The Constituency of Red Deer has the distinction of electing two Alberta Conservative leaders, Edward Michener and W.J.C. "Cam" Kirby to the Legislature.

A total of twelve men have represented this constituency in the Legislature.

In the first general election held in November 1905, John T. Moore, the wealthy president of the Central Alberta Railway, was elected by defeating Rev. Leo Gaetz, the founder of the city of Red Deer. He sat in the House for four years.

In 1909, Michener was elected as an Independent. Later, he joined the Conservative caucus. In 1910, when R.B. Bennett quit provincial politics to go federal, he was named his successor as the Alberta Conservative leader.

In 1917, Michener came close to toppling the Liberal government. It was said Premier Sifton saved his administration by first passing a special Act of the Legislature to permit the twelve members in the Canadian Army to be re-elected by acclamation, and secondly, by creating two special seats for soldiers and nurses serving in Europe. It was a known fact that servicemen were pro-conservatives. In the federal election held the same year, soldiers voted in their home ridings. In Edmonton West, Conservative General W.A. Griesbach was trailing Liberal Frank Oliver by 80 votes after the civil votes were counted. Griesbach obtained 2,938 militia ballots, compared to Oliver's 160 ballots. The final results of this election left the Liberals with 34 seats, an overall majority of ten. This was the closest Alberta has been to having a minority government in seventy-seven years! Michener was named to the Senate the next year.

In the resulting by-election, J.J. Gaetz, the nephew of Rev. Leo Gaetz, was elected.

Three members for Red Deer have died while still in the House. They were UFA-er G.W. Smith in 1931; former MP Alfred Speakman , the leader of the official opposition in 1943; and Social Crediter David Ure in 1954.

In the February 1954 by-election Conservative Red Deer lawyer Kirby was elected and four years later he was chosen the first Alberta Conservative leader for twenty years. He lost his seat in 1959 general election that saw only one Conservative elected, even though the party obtained 26 percent of the popular vote. In 1961, Kirby was appointed to the Alberta Supreme Court Trial Division.

The Constituency of Ribstone

The former constituency of Ribstone was created in the redistribution prior to the 1913 general election. The romantic name "Ribstone" first appears on Palliser's Map of the Canadian prairies, published in 1865 and may refer to a large erratic rock that bears marks resembling a man's ribs, that is located on the open plain south of Wainwright.

Four men were elected for this constituency during the twenty-seven years that it appeared on provincial electoral division maps. The first was Liberal James Gray Turgeon. Born in 1879 at Bathurst, New Brunswick, he was the son of Senator Onesiphore Turgeon. Educated at Bathurst, he came to Alberta as a young man and became a prominent Edmonton stock broker, who had residence in Hardisty. He entered the Legislature by defeating William J. Blair, who later was elected the Member of Parliament for Battle River. He sat in the House for eight years. He is remembered as being most unhappy about the Act to give women the right to vote. He died in 1964 as a Senator at the age of eighty-five.

In the UFA sweep of 1921, C.B.F. Wright was elected by defeating Turgeon. He died less than a year later. In the resulting by-election W.G. Farquharson, the UFA candidate was elected over Liberal Edmonton businessman J.J. McKenna. He sat in the House for thirteen years as a private member. Farquharson was a wealthy Ontario-born Provost farmer.

In the 1935 general election, Social Crediter A.L. Blue was elected by a large majority over Liberal R.M. Lee. Farquharson came in a poor third. Blue joined the insurgents in the ill-fated rebellion of SoCred back benchers that attempted to topple Premier Aberhart's government in the spring of 1937. Blue with Barner, Cockroft and MacLellan crossed the floor of the Legislative and sat as Independent Progressive.

The constituency disappeared in the 1940 redistribution being merged into Wainwright and Sedgewick. Blue took this personally. He contested Wainwright unsuccessfully as an Independent Social Craditer in the general election of that year, but only received 365 of the 5,301 votes cast.

These men who represented Ribstone in the Legislature should be remembered as public spirited men of ability.

The Former Constituency of Rocky Mountain
1909 – 1940

The Constituency of Rocky Mountain (not to be confused with Rocky Mountain House) first appeared on the Alberta Electoral Division Map in 1909. It was created by joining the coal mining area of the Crowsnest Pass with the holiday resort of Banff.

The first mention of the name "Rocky Mountains" is to be found in the Legardeur St. Pierre's Journal for 1752, in which he says he has seen the 'Montagnes de Roche' after crossing the plains from Portage La Prairie.

The vast, new constituency stretched from the international boundary to a hundred miles of north of Canmore. The majority of voters were miners. A total of five men represented Rocky Mountain in the twenty-nine years of its existence. The first member was Charles M. O'Brien, a full-time organizer for the Socialist party of Canada. He is remembered today as still holding the record of delivering the longest speech that lasted more than eight hours. He was an authority of Karl Marx's Dor Kajnatal. He sat in the House for four years before being defeated.

In 1913, long-time pioneer mountain guide Robert E. Campbell was elected with a 99 vote majority. He ran as an Independent and later joined the Conservative caucus. At the outbreak of World War I, he joined the Canadian Army and served as a Captain with the 192nd Battalion on the Western Front. He sat for Rocky Mountain for eight years, and then contested unsuccessfully Clearwater in 1921. Later, he became a prominent Calgary grain dealer.

The next member was Philip Martin, a Blairmore miner, who held the seat for nine years in the years he sat as one of the six Labor members. There has never since been such a large group of Labor members in the Legislature.

In 1930, the constituency returned George Cruickshank, an Independent who was a prominent Hillcrest merchant. He sat in the House for five years.

The last member to be elected for Rocky Mountain before it was abolished was Social Crediter Lawrence Duke. Born in Ontario, he was educated at Orangeville before attending the Calgary Normal School. He taught in Camrose for a number of years besides working for three years in the Anglican Mission at Moose Factory, James Bay. In 1940, Duke was re-elected for Pincher Creek/Crowsnest and sat in the House for a total of thirteen.

The Constituency of Rocky Mountain House
1940 – 1980

The Constituency of Rocky Mountain House was created prior to the 1940 general election by cutting off western rural half of the old Red Deer riding. The centre of the population is the town of Rocky Mountain House, which was close to 4,000 residents. It was the site of a North West Company trading post as early as 1799 and remained a Hudson bay Company post until 1875. Although lumbering used to be the chief industry of the area, farming is now the main occupation.

The first member for Rocky Mountain House was Social Crediter Alfred Hooke, who had previously represented Red Deer in the Legislature. Born in England, he came to Alberta as a child with his parents. Educated at Stettler, he attended the University of Alberta before becoming a school teacher. Young Hooke taught school – first at Trochu for ten years, and then at Rocky Mountain House for five. He was the last of the original Social Crediters of "The Class of 1935" to sit in the Legislature. He retired in 1971 after thirty-six years of public service.

He was a prominent member of the group of SoCred back benchers called "the insurgents", who unsuccessfully attempted to force Premier Aberhart to resign the premiership and give it to Dr. Harvey Brown in the spring of 1937.

In 1943, when Manning became premier, he appointed Hooke the Provincial Secretary. He also served as Minister of Economic Affairs, Public Welfare and Lands and Forests at one time or another during the next twenty-four years. He withdrew at the last minute from contesting the Social Credit leadership when Manning retired in 1968.

Premier Harry Strom did not include him in his cabinet. Hooke spent his last three years in the Legislature as a private member. He did not seek re-election in 1971.

The next member was Mayor Helen Hunley of Rocky Mountain House, who sat in the Legislature for eight years. She served in the cabinet, first as a Minister without Portfolio and then in 1973 as the Solicitor General. Two years later, she was transferred to the department of Social Services and Community Health. She did not seek re-election in 1979, but retired from politics at the age of fifty-nine.

The present member is Conservative Jack Campbell, a Caroline farmer, who had a vote majority over SoCred Lavern Ahlstrom in the 1982 general election. He is part president of The Canadian Sheep Breeder Association.

The Constituency of St. Paul
1913 -1982

The Constituency of St. Paul was created prior to the 1913 general election. A total of seven residents have represented this constituency north of the North Saskatchewan River in the Alberta Legislature. The main centre is the town of St. Paul with a population of 4,500/ in 1896, Father Lacombe, OMI, established a missionary Metis settlement. After twelve years, the project was abandoned and the area opened up for homesteaders. Today, about half of the population is of French Canadian origin. In recent decades, a large number of Ukrainian Canadians have moved into the region.

In 1913, Prosper-Edmond Lessard, the former Liberal member for Pakan, was elected, defeating Conservative Laurent Garneu by 90 votes. Lessard (1873 – 1930) was a successful Edmonton wholesale merchant. He married into the prominent Gariepy family. He sat as the member of St. Paul, until he was defeated by Laudas Joly, the UFA candidate in 1921. Four years later, he was appointed a Senator.

Joly held the seat for nine years. Born in Quebec, he was the descendent of D'Aille'-bost, a governor under the French regime. He was educated at the University of Ottawa before coming to Alberta in 1908. He was a prominent St. Paul farmer. In 1952, he successfully came out of political retirement and was elected the Social Credit member for Bonnyville.

In the 1930 general election, Joseph Dechene had been the Liberal member for Beaver River in the early 1920s who was elected. Born in Quebec, Dechene's ancestors had settled in New France in 1623. He also married into the prominent Gariepy family. He was a pioneer farmer in the Bonnyville district. He did not hold his seat in the 1935 Social Credit sweep. Five years later, he contested successfully the federal riding of Athabasca and sat in the Commons until he retired from politics at the advanced age of seventy-nine in 1958. Many believe that Joseph Dechene was the "smartest politician" Alberta has yet produced.

Social Crediter Joseph Beaudry represented St. Paul from 1935 to 1952.

When he retired, he was replaced by another Social Crediter Ray Reierson, a St. Paul automobile and agricultural implement dealer. Born at Edberg of Danish parents, he enlisted in the Canadian Army at the outbreak of the Second World War. He served in Europe as a captain. Premier Manning named him to the cabinet as the Minister of Labor in 1955. After Educational Minister Randy MacKinnon was defeated in 1967, he was transferred to Department of Education. A year later, Premier Strom re-appointed him Minister of Labor, even though he was one of the unsuccessful candidates in the leadership race to replace Manning. Reierson retired from politics after being defeated at the polls in 1971.

The first Conservative to represent St. Paul was Mick Fluker, a St. Paul auctioneer, who held the seat from 1971 to 1979.

The member in the Legislature was Dr. Charles Anderson, who had a 319 vote majority over Laurent Dubois, the NDP candidate. Born in 1942 in Vulcan, Anderson was educated at Milo before qualifying as a medical doctor at the University of Alberta. He is an active member of the Church of Jesus Christ of Latter Day Saints. Even though he moved permanently to the United States in 1971, he did not resign his seat to the Legislature. Dr. Anderson has announced he will not be a candidate in the November 2nd general election.

The Constituency of Sedgewick
1909 – 1979

The Constituency of Sedgewick first appeared on the Alberta Electoral Map in 1909 and disappeared seventy years later. It was named after Mr. Justice Robert Sedgewick (1848 – 1906), who, after serving as federal Deputy Minister of Justice, was appointed to the Supreme Court of Canada.

A total of six men have represented this constituency in the Legislature. The first was the third Premier of the province, Charles Stewart. He was a prominent Killam farmer. After being elected for Sedgewick in 1909, he sat for thirteen years in the House. Premier Sifton named him Minister of Public Works in 1913; four years later, he became the Premier.

In the 1921 general election, Premier Stewart was again elected by acclamation even though his government was defeated by the United Farmers. A year later, he resigned his seat to successfully enter federal politics. Stewart was the federal Minister of Interior from 1921 to 1930. His son, Charles Stewart, is incumbent P.C. member for Wainwright.

The second member was A.G. Andrews, who was elected by acclamation in the 192 by-election. Born in England, he taught for years in Alberta before becoming a successful Sedgewick farmer. He sat in the House for fourteen years.

In the 1935 general election, Social Crediter Albert F. Fee defeated Andrews. He was a Killam undertaker and hardware dealer who had served as a councillor. He sat for seventeen years in the House as a private member before retiring at the age of sixty-six.

In 1952, SoCred Jack Hillman replaced Fee. Born in England, he was educated in Ohio before coming to Alberta as a young man. He became a prosperous Forestburg farmer. Hillman sat in the House for nineteen years before retiring from politics at the advanced age of eighty-four.

In 1971, the Social Credit retained Sedgewick when Ralph Sorenson, a Killam farmer and rancher, was elected. He sat on the opposition benches in the House for four years. He failed in his re-election bid.

The last member of Sedgewick was the present Minister of Transportation, Henry Kroeger. After running as a Liberal in the 1950s, he joined the Conservatives. He is a Consort implement dealer.

Many Albertans were saddened when the Redistribution Commission announced that the constituency of Sedgewick would be abolished.

The Constituency of Smoky River
1971 – 1982

The Constituency of Smoky River was created prior to the 1971 general election. The name came from the Smoky River, a tributary of the Peace, which forms the western border of the constituency. The name is derived from the fact that smoldering coal beds along the riverbanks results in a perpetual haze or mist during most of the year, especially during the autumn months.

The man that has represented Smoky River in the Legislature for the past eleven years is Marvin Moore. He is one of the ablest members in Premier Lougheed's Cabinet and a possible contender to be his successor. Born in 1938 at Grande Prairie, Moore was educated there. He is now a successful DeBolt farmer and business man, and came from a prominent old Social Credit family.

In 1975, Premier Lougheed named him to the Cabinet as the Minister of Agriculture. For the past three years, he has been the Minister of Municipal Affairs. In the 1979 general election, Moore was elected with a 1,200 vote majority over his nearest opponent Anne Hemingway of the NDP. Moore was re-elected in 1982.

The Constituency of Spirit River
1940 – 198

The large Northern Alberta Constituency of Spirit River was created prior to the 1940 general election. It was renamed Spirit River/Fairview in 1970, when its boundaries were changed. Its western boundary is the British Columbia border and it lies between the 20th Base Line and the 24th Base Line, while Cardinal Lake is the easterly point. The two centers of large population are Fairview with 2,600 residents and the town of Spirit River with just over 1,000 residents. This part of the Peace River block was the last part of the province to welcome homesteaders in the 1920s.

The first member to be elected to the Legislature was SoCred Henry DeBolt, an early pioneer. The hamlet, population 63, of DeBolt was named after him in 1923, as he was the first postmaster. He sat in the Legislature as a private member for twelve years.

The next member to be sent to Edmonton was Adolphe Olaf Fimrite, long-time proprietor of a department store in Wanhom. He represented the constituency for nineteen years. In 1963, he was named Deputy Chairman of the Northern Alberta Development Council and three years later Premier Manning took him into the cabinet as a Minister without Portfolio. He was re-appointed to the cabinet by Premier Strom in 1968. Fimrite was forced to retire from politics when he was defeated at the polls in 1971.

The incumbent member for Spirit River/Fairview is the Alberta leader of the NDP, Grant Notley, who has held the seat for the past eleven years. Born in 1939 at Didsbury, he was educated at schools in Westerdal, Olds and Didsbury. As a teenager, he suffered from an embarrassing stutter. He became active in the CCF youth movement while a student on the University of Alberta campus in the late 1950s. He went on to help organize the New Democratic Party in the province in the early 1960s. In 1962, Notley was chosen the NDP Provincial Secretary, a position he held for the next six years. He assisted in the election of Garth Turcott in the 1966 Pincher Creek/Crowsnest by-election.

In 1968, the leader of the Alberta NDP, Neil Reimer, retired and Notley was chosen to replace him while still only thirty years of age.

He contested unsuccessfully first Edmonton Norwood in 1967 and then the Edson 1969 by-election. In the 1971 general election, he was victorious in Spirit River/Fairview, winning by a narrow 54 vote margin. In 1979, Notley had close to a 1,000 vote majority over his nearest opponent Tory Mayor Jim Reynolds of Spirit River.

In 1982, Notley was re-elected and in 1983 named the Leader of the Opposition in the Legislature.

The Former Constituency of Sturgeon

The Constituency of Sturgeon, located north and east of Edmonton, was one of the original 25 Electoral Divisions into which the new province was divided in 1905. Many of the residents were recently arrived homesteaders and settlers from Ontario or the United States. It existed for thirty-five years before disappearing from the Alberta Electoral Map.

Three men represented Sturgeon in the Legislature; John R. Bogle from 1905 to 1921; Samuel Carson and James M. Popil. In 1894, Bogle came to the North West Territories to teach at Regina. He later qualified as a lawyer and moved to Edmonton. He served as an Edmonton alderman before entering the Legislature. He was named the Deputy Speaker in 1906. Bogle was one of the leading "insurgents" Liberals that forced Premier Rutherford to resign.

Premier Sifton took him into the Cabinet as Minister of Education in 1913. Premier Stewart appointed him the Attorney General in 1918. In the 19221 general election, he contested two seats – Sturgeon, where he was defeated, and Edmonton, where he was elected. He was the leader of the official Opposition in the Legislature when he was appointed a Justice of the Alberta Supreme Court's Trial Division. Mr. Justice Bogle died in 1936 at the age of fifty-six.

In 1921, Carson, a Namao farmer, was elected and sat as the UFA member for Sturgeon for fourteen years. He then retired from politics at the age of sixty-five.

The last member was James M. Popil, who ran unsuccessfully as a Conservative candidate in 1930 and successfully as a Social Crediter five years later. In 1940,

Popil was returned as the member for Redwater. He sat in the House until he retired from politics in 1948 at the age of thirty-nine. Born of Ukrainian parents in Redwater, Popil qualified as a teacher. He first ran for the House when he was only twenty-one.

These three men served the residents of Sturgeon well in the Legislature and should be remembered as members of the group of pioneers who helped to make Alberta what she is today.

The Constituency of Taber/Warner
1913 – 1982

The Southern Alberta Constituency of Taber/Warner, located east and south of Lethbridge, was originally formed in 1909 and known as Lethbridge District. In the general election that year, two Liberals, the official Liberal candidate Dr. J.H. Rivers of Raymond, and Independent Liberal A.J. McLean (1860 – 1933) who was a Purple Spring rancher, contested the seat. McLean won and was accepted into the Liberal caucus. A year later, he was taken into Premier Sifton's cabinet as the Provincial Secretary.

Prior to 1913, Lethbridge was split into two constituencies; Taber in the north and Warner in the south. They were to be rejoined in 1963.

During the next fifty years, there were six members elected to represent Taber in the Legislature. McLean held the seat for eight years. In 1921, he was defeated by UFA Lawrence Peterson, a Barnwell Mormon farmer, who was the chairman of the Taber Irrigation District. Peterson failed to win his party's nomination in 1930.

The next member was J.J. McLellan, a wealthy Purple Spring farmer. He served briefly in Premier Reid's cabinet.

In 1935, Taber went Social Credit, electing James Hanse, a Danish-born Mormon farmer, who was the Mayor of Taber. He did not seek re-election in 1940. His place in the Legislature was taken by SoCred Roy. S. Lee (1887 – 1982), who held the seat for the next twenty-three years. In 1955, Lee was involved in "the Lee-Lander you" scandal and was expelled from the Social Credit party on the eve of the election. Both ran as Independent Social Crediters and were re-elected. They were later readmitted to the Social Credit caucus. In 1963, when Taber was joined to neighboring Warner, Lee retired from politics at the age of seventy-six.

The first member of the Warner constituency was Liberal Leffingwell, an American born hotel proprietor.

In 1921, the constituency went UFA, returning Maurice Connor, an American born Warner farmer, who had been a Methodist minister for eighteen years. He sat in the Legislature for fourteen years. Connor's daughter, Dorothea Jean, married Deane Gundlock, the Member of Parliament for Lethbridge from 1958 to 1972.

The seat was captured by SoCred Solon Low, a Stirling High School principal, in 1935. He entered Premier Aberhart's cabinet as the Provincial Treasurer in 1937. He was the only cabinet Minister to be defeated in 1940. Independent James Walker (1895 - 1954), an American born business executive with the Raymond Knight Sugar Company edged pass Low with a 379 majority. Walker had been unsuccessful UFA candidate five years previously. He went on to become the leader of the twenty-seven member strong official opposition.

However, Walker was defeated by Low, who was by then the Minister of Education in 1944. The next year, Low resigned the seat to enter federal politics and was elected the SoCred Member of Parliament for Peace River. He sat in the Commons for thirteen years as the National Leader of the Social Credit movement.

In the 1945 by-election, SoCred Leonard Halmrast was elected and represented Warner, then Taber/Warner for the next twenty-two years. Halmrast (1899 - 1979), an

American born Milk River farmer, served in the cabinet for fourteen years, most of it of which he was the Minister of Agriculture. He has the distinction of being the last member of the Legislature to be elected by acclamation. This occurred in 1963. He retired from politics four years later at the age of sixty-eight.

The next member to represent this constituency was SoCred Doug Miller, a former Mayor of Taber. Miller (1904 - 1982), who was a brother-in-law of Roy S. Lee, was a Cinema owner and operator. He retired from politics in 1975 at the age of seventy.

The present incumbent member for Taber/Warner is Tory Minister of Social Services and Community Health "Bob" Bogle. He ran unsuccessfully against SoCred Miller in 1971, while a Milk River town councillor. Four years later, he entered the Legislature by defeating the Social Credit leader at that time, Warner Schmidt. He entered Premier Lougheed's cabinet as the Minister responsible for Native Affairs in 1975. Bogle is a former high school teacher.

The Constituency of Three Hills
1963 – 1982

The Constituency of Three Hills was created prior to the 1963 general election. The town of Three Hills, with a population close to 2,000, is the largest centre. The well-known Prairie Bible Institute, a non-denominational educational institution on fundamental lines that prepare Protestant foreign Missionaries, is located there.

A total of four men and one woman has represented this constituency in the Legislatures in Edmonton in the last nineteen years. The first member elected was Social Crediter L. Petrie Weston, but he died in November 1963 before taking his seat in the legislature.

In the resulting January 1964 by-election, Social Crediter Roy Davidson, a fifty-seven year old farmer, was elected by a 419-vote margin, defeating the Liberal Alberta leader David Hunter. Davidson sat in the Legislature for three years.

In the 1967 general election, SoCred Ray Ratzlaff, a thirty-six year old teacher, was elected. Premier Strom named him to the cabinet in 1969 as the Minister of industry and tourism. Ratzlaff went down to defeat in the first Lougheed sweep of 1971.

The fourth member for Three Hills was Dr. Allan "Landslide" Warwick. He defeated Ratzlaff by the narrow margin of eight votes, hence his nickname. Born in 1937 at Calgary, he was educated at Langdon and Strathmore before attending Olds School of Agriculture. He then attended both the University of Alberta and Iowa State University, receiving a Doctoral degree from the latter. An agricultural economist,

Dr. Warwick was on the University of Calgary academic staff when elected. He was the first active Universe professor to become a member of the Legislature since 1905. Premier Lougheed named him to the cabinet as the Minister of Lands and Forests. In 1975, he was transferred to the Utilities portfolio. He retired from politics in 1979 at the age of forty-two.

The present member in the Legislature is Connie Osterman, a Carstairs farmer, who was an active Liberal before becoming a conservative.

The Constituency of Victoria
1905 – 1940

The Constituency of Victoria was one of the original 25 Electoral Divisions that the newly created province of Alberta was divided into, prior to the first general election. At this time, large numbers of new Canadians were coming in from Eastern Europe and taking up homesteads in the area east of Edmonton. Many were called "Ruthenians", or Ukrainians. The constituency existed for thirty-five years until it was abolished prior to the 1940 general election.

A total of five persons represented Victoria in the Legislature. In 1905, Frank A. Walker, the Liberal candidate was elected, defeating Conservative John W. Shera, who had been the member of this district in the NWT Assembly at Regina. He sat in the House for sixteen years until he was defeated in 1921. Born in 1871 in Middlesex County, Ontario, he was educated at Winnipeg. Coming to Alberta with his father in 1883, he travelled across the prairie beyond Crowfoot Crossing, which was the farthest point in the railway tracks had been laid. He later homesteaded near Fort Saskatchewan. At the outbreak of World War I, walker enlisted in the Canadian Army and saw active service as Major on the Western Front. He retired from faming in 1926 and moved to Vancouver. When he died in 1956, he was the last surviving member of the first Alberta Legislature.

In 1921, William Fedun was elected as the UFA member for Victoria. He sat in the House for five years.

The third member was Rudolph Henning, who sat for Victoria from 1925 to 1930, and then was elected for Clover Bar. Born in Russia of German ancestry, he came to Canada as a child. He became a successful farmer and served as a school trustee for twenty years.

In 1930, Peter Miskew was elected by a narrow 66-vote margin. He had come to Canada with his parents from Russia in 1902. The family settled near Mundare. He attended the University of Alberta, graduating in Arts before training as a teacher. Miskew was the principal for a number of years. He sat in the House for five years.

The last person to represent this constituency was Social Crediter Samuel Calvert, an Ontario-born former blacksmith pioneer Victoria farmer. Calvert was the constituency's Returning Officer from 1900 to 1905. He also served as Mayor of Chipman, and eventually retired from politics in 1940 at the age of seventy-three.

The five men who served the residents of Victoria in the Legislature in the early days should be remembered as public-spirited men of ability.

The Constituency of Vermillion
1905 – 1982

The Constituency of Vermillion has the distinction of electing two members who have become premiers of Alberta. The first was Arthur Sifton, who served as president of the Executive Council from 1910 to 1917 and the second was Richard Gavin Reid, the UFA Premier for a year in 1913. In all, ten men have represented this constituency.

In 1905, Liberal pioneer Matthew McCauley was elected. He had homesteaded near Fort Saskatchewan in 1879 and later became a successful contractor and deliveryman. He had served a term as the member for Edmonton in the NWT Legislature in Regina. He also served eighteen years as an Edmonton school trustee. McCauley resigned his seat in order to become the warden of the Edmonton Penitentiary. Later, he pioneered in the Peace River country, dying at Sexsmith at the age of eighty.

In the resulting by-election, Liberal James B. Holden, a Vegreville farmer and insurance agent was elected and sat for Vermillion and then Vegreville. In 1909, Archie Campbell was elected. He was an Innisfree farmer. Campbell resigned his seat to permit Premier Sifton to enter the Legislature. He sat for this constituency for seven years. Born in to one of the nation's most important political families, Sifton (1859 – 1921), was the elder brother of Sir Clifford Sifton. Manitoba born, he was educated at Cobourg's Victoria University before being called to the Manitoba Bar in 1883. He sat in the NWT Legislature for Banff before being appointed Chief Justice of the Territories.

In 1910, he retired from the Bench to become Alberta's second Premier. He led the Liberals to victory in the 1913 and the 1917 general elections.

In 1917, Premier Sifton, known as the "Sphynx", resigned his seat to join Prime Minister Bordon's wartime National government as Minster of Customs. He was a member of the Canadian delegation to the Versailles Peace Conference. He died suddenly in January 1921 at the age of sixty-two.

A retired Maritime Judge, A.W. Ebbett, held the seat for four years.

In the 921 United Farmers' of Alberta sweep, Vermillion retired R.G. Reid, a Scottish-born farmer, who served as Minister of health in Greenfield's cabinet. In 1926, Premier Brownlee appointed him the Provincial Treasurer. He held this post for eight years.

The UFA caucus chose Reid as Premier when Brownlee resigned in 1934. He was Alberta's fourth premier and held the position for only fourteen months. He went down to personal defeat in the 1935 general election that saw every UFA member defeated at the polls.

Vermillion's next member was Social Crediter William Fallow. Premier Aberhart appointed him the Minister of Public Works. In 1943, Aberhart passed away. Fallow lost out to Ernest Manning, when the SoCred caucus selected the young Trade and Industry Minster as the Premier.

Other Social Crediters who have been elected for Vermillion have been William R. Cornish (1944 – 1955) and Ashley Cooper (1955 – 1975).

The Constituency of Wainwright
1913 – 1982

The Constituency of Wainwright, located south of Lloydminster near the Saskatchewan border, first appeared on the 1913 Alberta Electoral Division Map. It was named after an executive of the Grand Trunk Pacific Railway.

A total of five men have represented this constituency in the Legislature in the last sixty-nine years. The first member was G. Leroy Hudson. At the outbreak of World War I, he joined the Canadian Army and saw active service as a Captain on the Western Front. He was re-elected in 1917 by a special Act of the Legislature. He sat a total of eight years as a Conservative.

In 1921, J. Russell Love, an Irma famer, defeated Major harry Strachan, VC by 964 votes. In 1934, Love was taken into Premier Reid's cabinet as the Provincial Treasurer. He sat in the House of fourteen years.

In 1935, Social Crediter William Masson was elected and sat for twenty years as a private member before retiring from politics at the age of sixty-seven.

His place was taken by SoCred Henry Ruste, who also sat for Wainwright for twenty years. He held two cabinet portfolios: Lands and Forests, and then Premier Strom's Minister of Agriculture from 1968 to 1971.

The member in the last Legislature was Conservative Charles Stewart, the grandson of Alberta's third Premier.

The Constituency of Whitford
1913 – 1940
& Willingdon
1940 – 1971

The Constituency of Whitford was created prior to the 1913 general election. The majority of residents were Ukrainian Canadian, who had only recently came from eastern Europe. Five Ukrainians were sent to represent the constituency in the Legislature in the next twenty-seven years. In 1940, the name of Whitford was changed to Willingdon in honor of a former Governor General of Canada, Freeman-Thomas, Marquis of Willingdon. This constituency in its turn, sent three individuals to the provincial house before it disappeared from the Alberta Electoral Division Map in 1971.

In 1913, Liberal Andrew Shandro was elected as the member for Whitford by edging out Paul Rudyk, the Ruthenian candidate. Born in 1886 in Bukowina, Shandro came to Alberta as a child with his parents and a group of relations. Educated at the Edmonton Business College, he became a federal government homestead inspector.

The courts nullified the election result because of action taken by Rudyk and declared the seat vacant.

A by-election was held in March 1915, which was won by Shandro. The Conservative candidate was Roman Kremer, an influential journalist.

In the 1917 general election, Shandro was re-elected by an Act of the Legislature, because he had briefly been in uniform. The other eleven members of the House, who were serving in the Canadian Army, were also returned to the

Legislature by this special Act. However, they were serving overseas.

Shandro's stormy political career continued in the 1921 general election, when the Whitford Returning Officer, Mr. Hawnelak, a relation, declared him elected by acclamation. Hawnelak rejected the UFA candidate Michael Chornhus' nomination papers on a technicality. Chornhus had typed his name with the final letter as an "S", while he wrote it with a "Z".

The courts again annulled this election. In the July 1922 by-election, Shandro was defeated by Chornhus. Shandro contested unsuccessfully Whitford in 1926 and again in 1935. He died in 1942 at Edmonton at the age of fifty-five. Chornhus, who did not have a good command of the English language, sat four years in the House and then retired.

In 1926, the constituency elected George M. Mihalcheon, the UFA candidate. Born in 1893 in Bukovina, he came to Alberta as a child and was educated at Vegreville before obtaining a teacher's certificate from the Camrose Normal School. After teaching for a number of years, he farmed near Boian and then became a general merchant. He sat in the Legislature for four years and then retired.

The next member was Tridone Goresky, a teacher who today is still alive and lives quietly in retirement in Edmonton. He sat in the House for five years.

In 1935, Social Crediter William Tomyn was elected the member for Whitford in a four way contest. Michael Nowakowski, the Communist candidate, was the runner up while Goresky came in third and Shandro came last. Tomyn sat for a total of twenty years in the Legislature for Whitford from 1935 to 1940, Willingdon from 1940 to 1952 and from 1959 to 1971 for Edmonton Norwood. Born in 1905 at Warwick, Alberta, he attended the Calgary Normal School and was a teacher for many years. He was active in Ukrainian cultural organizations. He died in 1972.

The second member for Willingdon was Nick Dushenski, who was the second CCF-er to be elected to the Legislature. He sat in the House from 1952 to 1959 when he retired from politics. After the 1955 general election, he was joined by another CCF-er Stand Ruzychi, who was the member for neighboring Vegreville. Both men were schoolteachers.

Willingdon's last member was Social Crediter Nick Melnyk. He sat for twelve years in the house as a private member. He was not a candidate in 1971, but retired from politics at the age of fifty-nine. Born at Kahwin, Alberta, he attended the Camrose Normal School before becoming the principal of Cadron School. In 1948, he moved to Andrew where he taught until he retired. In 1967, Melnyk was awarded the Centennial medal in recognition of his public service.

The eight Ukrainian Canadians, who served the residents of these two constituencies in the Legislature, should be remembered as public spirited men of ability.

The Constituency of Whitecourt
1971 – 1982

The Constituency of Whitecourt was created prior to the 1971 general election. The largest centre is the town of Whitecourt, population 4,000 on the Edmonton-Peace River Trail. The only member of the Legislature has been Conservative Peter Trynchy. Born in 1931 at Rockfort Bridge, Alberta, he is of Ukrainian descent. He is a Mayerthorpe businessman and farmer. He served on the town council for six years before entering provincial politics. He was a private member for eight years before he was taken into the cabinet as the Minister of Recreation and Parks.

In the last general election three years ago, Trynchy was elected with a 2,300-vote majority over his nearest opponent Ken Forscutt of the NDP.

About the Authors

Dr. Austin A. Mardon was born in Edmonton, the son of E.G. Mardon and May Mardon, an Edmonton teacher. Educated at Lethbridge, he did an M.A. at South Dakota State University and his Ph.D. at Greenwich University, Australia. He then served as a research scientist and participated in a meteorite recovery expedition in the late 1980's, spending some 50 days in a two-man tent 170 miles from the South Pole. He is a life member of the New York Explorer's Club.

His main work has been his humanitarian efforts with those suffering from schizophrenia and other mental illnesses. He has been active also with his father, Dr. Ernest G. Mardon, in authoring a score of books and academic articles, the latest of which is a series of historical studies of ethnic groups and Alberta politics. Dr. Mardon was appointed a member of the Order of Canada in 2007.

About the Editor

Aala Abdullahi is currently a Neuroscience student at the University of Alberta in Edmonton, Alberta.

www.ingramcontent.com/pod-product-compliance
Lightning Source LLC
Chambersburg PA
CBHW031555300426
44111CB00006BA/325